NOW

Brendan Kennelly was born in 1936 in Ballylongford, Co. Kerry, and was Professor of Modern Literature at Trinity College, Dublin from 1973 until his retirement in 2005. He has published more than 30 books of poetry, including *Familiar Strangers: New & Selected Poems 1960-2004* (2004). He is best-known for two controversial poetry books, *Cromwell*, published in Ireland in 1983 and in Britain by Bloodaxe in 1987, and his epic poem *The Book of Judas* (1991), which topped the Irish bestsellers list: a shorter version was published by Bloodaxe in 2002 as *The Little Book of Judas*. His third epic, *Poetry My Arse* (1995), did much to outdo these in notoriety. All these remain available separately from Bloodaxe, along with his other recent titles, *Glimpses* (2001), a collection of short poems, and *Martial Art* (2003), versions of the Roman poet Martial.

His latest poetry book *Now* (2006) is published simultaneously with *When Then Is Now* (2006), a trilogy of his modern versions of three Greek tragedies (all previously published by Bloodaxe): Sophocles' *Antigone* and Euripides' *Medea* and *The Trojan Women*. His *Antigone* and *The Trojan Women* was both first performed at Peacock Theatre, Dublin, in 1986 and 1993 respectively; *Medea* premièred in the Dublin Theatre Festival in 1988, toured in England in 1989 and was broadcast by BBC Radio 3. His other plays include Lorca's *Blood Wedding* (Northern Stage, Newcastle & Bloodaxe, 1996).

His translations of Irish poetry are available in *Love of Ireland: Poems from the Irish* (Mercier Press, 1989). He has edited several anthologies, including *The Penguin Book of Irish Verse* (1970/1981), *Between Innocence and Peace: Favourite Poems of Ireland* (Mercier Press, 1993), *Ireland's Women: Writings Past and Present*, with Katie Donovan and A. Norman Jeffares (Gill & Macmillan, 1994), and *Dublines*, with Katie Donovan (Bloodaxe Books, 1995). He has also published two novels, *The Crooked Cross* (1963) and *The Florentines* (1967).

His *Journey into Joy: Selected Prose*, edited by Åke Persson, was published by Bloodaxe in 1994, along with *Dark Fathers into Light*, a critical anthology on his work edited by Richard Pine. John McDonagh's critical study *Brendan Kennelly: A Host of Ghosts* was published in The Liffey Press's Contemporary Irish Writers series in 2004.

His cassette recordings include *The Man Made of Rain* (Bloodaxe, 1998) and *The Poetry Quartets: 4*, shared with Paul Durcan, Michael Longley and Medbh McGuckian (The British Council/Bloodaxe Books, 1999).

BRENDAN KENNELLY

NOW

BLOODAXE BOOKS

ISBN: 1 85224 748 7   hardback edition
       1 85224 749 5   paperback edition

First published 2006 by
Bloodaxe Books Ltd,
Highgreen,
Tarset,
Northumberland NE48 1RP.

www.bloodaxebooks.com
For further information about Bloodaxe titles
please visit our website or write to
the above address for a catalogue.

Bloodaxe Books Ltd acknowledges
the financial assistance of
Arts Council England, North East.

Cover design: Neil Astley & Pamela Robertson-Pearce.

Cover printing: J. Thomson Colour Printers Ltd, Glasgow.

Printed in Great Britain by
Bell & Bain Limited, Glasgow, Scotland.

And in today already walks tomorrow.

SAMUEL TAYLOR COLERIDGE (1772-1834)

NOW

What is 'now'? This moment, gone as soon as mentioned? Today? This week? Months? Year? Decade? Century? Or any and all of these? I don't know, but since many a good line of poetry springs from the interest born of the stimulating awareness of not knowing, I decided to write a poem sequence of three-liners that would try to capture the many sliding identities of 'now'. I wanted these little three-liners to dance with each other, and in that lively dance to express opinions, instant judgements, sudden memories, contradictions, jokes of the moment, rumours, echoes, proverbial voices, lines from diaries, phrases from newspapers, from conversations, from uninhibited gossip, from dreams, from the normal craziness and violence of daily life.

Time is a mere mite, an item. And the flashing character of 'now' demands a sharp form such as can be found in epigrams, proverbs, soundbites, heroic couplets (why 'heroic'?), witty bitchery, didya-hear-this one?, quotations tripping down the years, prayers, curses, words and phrases casually uttered and bemusedly overheard.

Miguel de Cervantes (1547-1616) said 'A proverb is a short sentence based on long experience'. For some fifty years now, I've been writing in different ways about time, most recently, for example, in *Cromwell*, *The Book of Judas*, *The Man Made of Rain* and *Martial Art*.

Now is an attempt to probe the concerns (obsessions?) with time in these poems in a more condensed, immediate way that is influenced by ancient proverbs from different cultures and modern headlines from different countries. Writers who are centuries apart echo each other in truly surprising ways. I see and hear that now.

NOW

Tinker is ten, thirty, fifty, eighty,
now and then and in between,
chained and free, lost and found, will be, is, has been.

The seagull lands on the window-sill,
assesses the man
alone in his cell.

The ambulance screams through the night.
Three o'clock. Loneliness
has a sleepless bite.

Now he sees a true friend is a challenge
and a shadowpresence guiding him
across a dangerous bridge.

He hears bottles breaking:
mad streets, shattered ideas, battered hearts,
bones creaking.

He hears the song he loves best
because more than anything or anyone
it promises rest.

Questions batter his head.
Cannibal answers
dance in his blood.

Now he longs for her caress
gentle, loving, naked.
His flesh is made of stress.

Now he sees Robert Emmet in Stephen's Green.
Two magpies play the happy game.
Soon, daffodils will dominate the scene.

He listens to the summoning bell.
If he answers what will he hear?
Talk of heaven? Song of hell?

He sees a colleague touch his side.
'Cancer,' he says. 'A few months.' The man
never lied.

He asks himself, what is a plan?
Is it something a man makes, or is it
what makes a man?

Now he hears of an old friend's death.
He sees him singing to the air
one glorious night in Merrion Square.

The Volvo misses him by inches.
The woman at the wheel smiles
as if she'd invited him to dinner.

He shivers at the forecast, same again:
windy, wet, cold.
Book a flight to the Age of Gold.

The druggie jumps through the window.
Blood swamps his head and face.
Tom Warner calls the police.

The blind woman kneels to pray,
her dog prone at her feet.
She is faithful to her way.

He picks a worm from the street,
gives it back to earth and grass.
When will his own home come to pass?

He finds a book, reads a page
he hadn't read for fifty years.
Nothing wrong with memory and tears.

The rugby pitch is embattled muck.
Filthy warriors win and lose.
Seagulls wait in hungry skies.

He watches Dante being translated.
Dante is embarrassed.
The translator is promoted.

He wonders why hate
has such an accomplished smile.
Hell is a paradise of style.

Now as he ponders the speed of light
the pain in his back
guarantees another sleepless night.

Now he sees true vanity
for the first time. The vain one
is a bubble through infinity.

Now he reads the honest letters of a man
who tells the famine as it was
and is. How does so much death live on?

He hears the bully taunt a friend
or one he thought was the bully's friend.
Will the bully ever have a friend?

He hears the magical strong song
of a tiny bird in Herbert Park.
Is this what makes the universe work?

He passes the redbricked house
where a country girl was murdered.
A perfect office now.

Now he hears how the shy man learned the trick
the first night of his honeymoon:
'Try the second hole down from the back o' the neck.'

Now he stands where a young man was hanged
millions of deaths ago.
He watches traffic flow jam flow stop flow.

She sits on the chapel steps in fine July,
opening her cup.
'You'll never feel down if you look up.'

His glasses fall and break.
Yes, of course he can see.
Mistake after mistake after mistake.

He knows that walls have ears
and voices too. 'What we say to him
will shortly be conveyed to you.'

Now he knows he's nothing:
Then, walking near the river, begins
to dream he may be something.

He recalls the words of Londoner Will Flint:
'You can say what you bloody well like, mate,
but beware of print!'

Her spirit begins to blush.
What's that in her hand?
A bomb or a brush?

He cannot remember her name.
Then he can. Then he cannot. He can. He cannot.
A time to love? A time to hate? A time to forget?

He watches feathers drifting
through the freezing air
like friends. From where? To where? Yes I do. I care.

He meets a friend with a broken jaw
and a black eye. Cheerful, though.
'Now and then, I fall outside the law.'

He meets an old friend, out of jail:
'I did as you said. I saw life from that window.
I owe my freedom to a seagull.'

Now he says 'now'. Say 'now', now is gone.
He's fond of his old clock.
Gutsy. Ticks on. On, Tinker, on.

He wonders why the night went so well.
Neither knew what the other meant.
Love is a happy accident.

Now he knows why Heather rejected him.
'Men who think too much are always broke,'
she said. 'I'd rather a pig in a poke.'

Now he sees that his real talent lies
in his ability to misunderstand
almost everything. Some surprising things, though, he can grasp.

He looks at the barman.
The spit of Einstein.
An expert on German wine.

He pays too much money
for a cup of coffee.
Rip-off Ireland is smart and grabby.

She shows him a long scar down her belly.
'I never met me mother,' she says.
'I never got love, though I give love gladly.'

He remembers the women gathered around the rock
of a man, and the girl happy to stroke
the wild hound's neck.

He's not afraid of being forgotten
because he knew, knows, men and women
(great, in their way) who embraced, embrace, oblivion.

She stuck her head down into the poem
and when she pulled her head back up
it knew new things about her lost home.

He hears a young woman
whisper to her mobile phone,
'No, I don't care, no, I'm not sad that she's gone!'

Now he sees seven daughters gather about their mother
who always made love in the grassy open air
because, she said, man's power meets God's blessing there.

He knows what it means to be invaded
but he will not surrender
to any sly attacker.

Tinker copes with pain.
It will go away.
It will come again.

All Tinker will do when the going gets rough
is close his eyes and say, 'There's a story
behind every pain.'

He listens to the latest statement
about killing, truth and justice.
Murder is what is lost in translation.

Tinker wonders at the man
whose ninetieth year has come and gone
and whose love of history is always young.

'I love growing old,' he says.
'I'm beginning to laugh at my past
and cherish my madness at last.'

'I love human dignity,' he smiles.
'It's life's ultimate prize.
Thank God for a child's eyes.'

He meets a man who has been
drunk for forty years.
Witty as ever. Laughing. Vengefully critical of others.

She sees him, says 'Hello'. Again, 'Hello'.
He says nothing. She says 'Your silence
is a perfect video.'

In a Barcelona café, he sits alone
sipping coffee. Is this true freedom, he wonders?
Are loneliness and freedom true brothers?

Walking streets he has never walked before
he thinks of friends long forgotten,
red apples in the hands of Patsy McGibbon.

Now he hears the children cry
when they hear the woman tell of the wave
drowning the sky.

He thinks of a powerful man
who strode the place with pride and style.
Went, one day. Never mentioned again.

In a sexy notebook, he writes one
sentence. Reads it aloud. Waits. Turns out the light.
Sits in the dark for hours. Is he alone?

Standing in rain, watching a worm
wriggling towards God knows what or where,
he anticipates the end of term.

He asks himself, why are they here?
The present is a question.
The future is not an answer.

Now he sees time dancing
to the music of itself
coming and going, going and coming.

The old tree gives a cheer:
on one of its bare branches glows
the first cherryblossom of the year.

Tinker thinks of now before any now began.
Sea, earth, trees, sky, clouds, ice, sun, rain.
No woman. No man.

For a tick, he thinks our stupidity
has brought all to the verge of destruction.
Grass and worms crave resurrection.

He recalls how he thought he'd never hear evil music
but he did, one night, between the sea and the street,
the dull stupid Dresden bombing of the devil's heartbeat.

Now he bows before the wonder of a smile,
one second, pure health for body and soul,
nothing more beautifully real.

He hears the young woman at the lecturer's door:
'Listen to the words he's using. I don't think
I understand English any more.'

She puts her question, 'Is it true that when
sober (as now) you are a likeable man,
and when drunk, a monstrous phenomenon?'

Education may be a gamble,
given all the talk of winners, losers.
He wants adventures, surprises, unexpected pleasures.

Now he thinks he has no right
to anything but the day's failures
and the lovely, black fragments of night.

Tinker hears a laugh from fifty years ago.
It flies across five decades,
a seagull over fields of snow.

After years of sorrow and fun,
he sees again the faces, hears the voices of those
who got the job done.

He thinks of a friend's father who said,
'Any day is good when you can wake up and put
one leg in front of the other.'

The girls pour from the Girls' School.
Who can ever do justice to this?
His shy words laugh and run away.

Now he wonders why his flesh is bruised,
twisting blueblack roads of hurt beneath the skin.
Yet he can't remember when the hurt began.

He remembers returning to consciousness,
his jaw smashed, his ribs crushing each other,
the warm body in the bed with him; his mother.

Leaving the room he thought was empty
he sees a body step out of the mirror,
begging him to return. He continues his journey.

Now he knows, listening to words of scorn
being poured on the man leaving for Australia
that no matter what he achieves he will never return.

Now he knows that certain of his words are closer
to each other than people can ever be.
He says words and people to himself, silently.

Now, after rain, in sunlight, jewels are everywhere,
yet he resists the greed to pick, pluck or steal one.
He takes to a street devoid of diamonds.

He listens to politicians. The radio
explodes with bullshit spreading
all over Europe.

She tells him she has given up smoking.
She has, however, put on four stone.
Chocolate. Sweet, sweet titbits. The lady is not for joking.

He listens to a man who knows when to be
silent. He listens to the silence and hears
a revealing story.

The beautiful hurt woman says she found a life of pain
because she swallowed a man's words, her heart
starlit with expectation.

Deborah Breen asks, 'How much of this scene,
this story, is made of lies?'
He lowers his eyes.

Now he is philosopher god hero gambler demon painter priest
and the whole universe.
Sometimes, bored or mad, or both, God help him, he writes verse.

He senses the extent of his own ignorance
and smiles at the thought that this may be the result
of a long and complex journey.

He sees an old friend howling at the moon.
After fifty years devoted to scholarship
he's howling at the moon.

Now it strikes him that some of the most brilliant
explainers of the arts and sciences
never reveal anything of themselves.

He meets a man he had met nearly
every day for thirty years. They both smile.
Neither knows the other's name.

In the darkness he opens his eyes,
looks out the midnight window
at heaven's spies.

His mind feels so timid and small
he wonders if it is
a mind at all.

Now a teacher tells him that in her school
most of the kids are on drugs
and live on another planet.

The seagull drifts through the sky
with a careless joy almost lost to humans
hurrying by.

The Angelus bell pacifies the air
where the seagull's cries
are a wild prayer.

'Happiness! Happiness! Happiness!
Well, yes, I could be worse,
more or less.'

Now his mind is mad, so mad
it flirts with midges, dances with snakes
Patrick failed to banish.

He watches heaven's spies slide into hiding.
He'll wait, see them re-emerge, vigilant,
bright and smiling.

He hears how a poet faded away,
lost his voice shaking hands with important folk
and perished of diplomacy.

Now, again, he sits in the dark for hours
until the voices come, laughing, challenging,
daring him with 'Listen! Listen! Write us down.'

Now the challenges have wings, they know
they can explore the blackbird's throat
and tell the darkness how it sings.

Now the mind-boulders are pushed aside
and for a moment it seems as though
he has never lied.

In the first morning light he cries
and can't say why. A voice asks
'Do dreams lie?'

Now he leaps over decades to find
a friend at a fountain, his body bruised,
hatred of school in his heart and mind.

Now the old teacher's name is mentioned.
The young priest's face hardens. Where
is forgiveness now?

He quits the city crowds,
sits alone in a quiet place
and studies faces in the clouds.

The jibes return, mocking mouths, sneering eyes,
part of the scene, of course, forever part of the scene
and will be, will be, as they have always been.

An angry woman asks, 'How many of us
use the system to promote ourselves?' Faltering,
he doesn't reply. Later, in darkness, he wonders why.

He looks into the pit of his own emptiness.
Hugely dark down there.
He ups his eyes. Seagulls bless the air.

He kicks his mind with the question:
what if the whole story was told
and every thought was known?

He thinks of the word that scares him most.
Even its flashing shadow terrifies,
or the thought of that word as a ghost.

At the telling of Christ's betrayal, the lovers kiss.
Surely if there's an answer to betrayal,
it's this.

A voice says, 'Follow where it leads you.'
What? Where? Does he like being led?
Yes. Therefore, he chooses a road through his head.

Now he thinks he may begin to understand time.
Some roads go where time is slow to go.
A voice says, 'Add a k to now, now you know.'

Now she recovers from a long illness and names
College friends and lovers from forty years ago.
Her eyes are shining, her voice magically low.

He listens to a speaker
who has run out of something to say.
He hears a voice caught between a curse and a prayer.

Tears in his eyes, the old teacher repeats
the same line to the enchanted young:
'And the birds go to sleep by the sweet wild twist of her song.'

Love enters his voice, he hears himself
saying things he never thought he'd say.
Surprise brings silence, love has had its way.

Now he thinks, 'If I could only scrub the shit
out of my mind as that woman scrubs the loo
I might be both Houyhnhnm and Yahoo.'

He looks at the loved books in the room.
They are part of him now and for life
but he'll never be part of them.

He sees a seven-year-old friend
crying, hands bruised, in the corner of the playground:
'I'd love never to read a line again!'

The book-lover stands at the bookshop window
staring in a way that says he'd be happy
to stand and stare forever.

Now, aged ten, he stumbles on *Paradise Lost*
in a laneway, and starts to read.
Heaven and Hell clash and dance in his head.

Now he hears the censor speak:
'They were different times. Someone had to decide.
Yes, I know why the young poet died.'

He sees the old novelist sway
from pub to pub, from street to street:
'I'm no Dickens, lad! He made ends meet!'

Near the top of the ladder, the painter
explodes but doesn't fall:
'These fuckin' mickeymouse jobs, I hate 'em all!'

Deborah Breen goes jogging along the canal.
Even the swans are watchful.
Tinker is grateful.

He follows a word that follows him.
He's catching up, the word swerves, vanishes
into a swan's wing.

He hears a voice poised between hope
and despair. Echoes, shadows, confessions
spread everywhere.

After forty years teaching, he wonders
who is a teacher? What he hates most
is dubbing someone a failure.

The true severity of love hits his heart,
the warm attentive clouds fragment
and drift away to play another part.

Now he knows what jealousy is
or thinks he does.
Is the nettle jealous of the rose?

How can such enraged passion,
based on a false perception,
devour the heart and soul of a decent man?

A stranger tells him how
his girlfriend hanged herself
and why he'll never know why.

Now, in his mind, he clouds away
yet doubts there is much
he'll leave behind.

He knows he lives in an age of money.
Has there ever been a different age?
Does education serve this clever slavery?

He ponders the old soldier:
'Only the rebel and the wise lover
know the right moment to surrender.'

Now he wonders who said, 'I was deeply moved
by the tragic shabbiness of this
sinister country.'

The botanist kneels before the flowers,
touches them as though in prayer.
If love is paying attention, love is here.

In hot July, the old man warns
the student of agriculture:
'Summer is not for ever. Build barns.'

He reads a poem aloud, with love and care.
Days later, he listens to it, out there,
total poem living in the air.

Now an old, old story
happens again.
A goddess sleeps with a man.

Now he is visited by another
ghost. All right, so it's only fifty years
since he saw that laughing lover.

He acknowledges the playful spirit
of time. Sometimes, lying alone, tired of work,
he hears it laughing in the dark.

The educational value of pain
teaches him to be alone,
a state in which he feels free to moan.

Now he turns youth and age upside down:
a rheumatic infant
turns to a howling clown.

The drinker, trying to balance pleasure with pain,
finds they're inseparable.
He drinks his fill.

The student pretends to tremble, cough,
vomit. The teacher says, 'What's wrong? Can I help?'
The student says, 'Fuck off!'

Now, from a train, Tinker sees a naked woman
running through a field. She's breaking
all the records.

Now the lost brother says he wanders, wanders
endlessly because his lost eyes need
the foreign challenge of surprise.

Tinker reads a sentence from fourteen
hundred years ago
and smiles to feel his blood's quick, youthful flow.

The magician's fingers move with such speed
and skill they twinkle and laugh
at a boy's innocent greed.

He knows his broken sleep is never surprising,
unlike the smell of freshcut March grass.
The dawn never grows tired of rising.

The happy scientist laughs, 'Hark! Hark!
A good poet has the mind of a magpie,
and sometimes, the throat of a lark!'

Now he dreams of mercy. Why?
Because a child hiding behind a nameless tree
begins to cry.

A question leaps from every scarred bone:
is there anyone in all the hurrying crowd
who is not alone?

Now he thinks the problem with now is that it thinks
it knows much more than then.
He reads papers. Listens to Amergin.

He listens to the News:
murder, robbery, war, corruption, disease, famine, rape,
prisoners on the roof. No escape.

The loving magic in this woman's eyes
– she must be eighty – surpasses all the promises
in the talk of progress.

He places money in the cap
of the young man spreading magic
from his violin in Grafton Street.

Now he knows so much has been lost
it will take a team of active dreamers
to recover a true fragment.

Now may be, in the long history
of self-deception, the most convincing moment.
Earthquakes are honesty.

Looking at the long procession, he thinks
of the tongue in every mouth. Silent now.
But, dear God, the explosions tonight at dinner.

It's near midnight. The city yawns.
Clocks persist. Lovers too. Churches. Big closed doors.
Christ goes walking. Screams die out. But not whispers.

Now the moon interviews him.
The most searing questions he has ever heard.
He'd like his answers to be profound. Absurd.

The light dances with darkness
to a music that enchants his heart
though his heart is the floor they dance on.

He hears the voice of his loved Einstein:
'I think in music. I live my daydreams in music.
I don't care for money. I love my work. I love my violin.'

Now he hears the voice in distant music:
'Knowledge is limited.
Imagination encircles the world.'

He meets a tattered man who was
a brilliant student thirty years ago. Wants five euro
for a hostel. If not five then, please, one or two.

He meets a polished fake who always knew
how to do exams. Such charm! Such concerns!
And all those funny quotes from Robbie Burns!

Now he asks, 'Who are you, Tinker? Who are you now?'
He listens, swallows his tears, laughing
and wipes the sweat from his brow.

He gets off a train in Amsterdam.
An elegant stranger walks up to him and says,
'A throwaway thing you said helped me be the man I am.'

Now puffs the man with the pipe in his mouth,
hands in his pockets; in thirty years
Tinker never saw him without it.

The old man says, 'Wisdom is worth stealing
by and from any man. But make sure
you pass it on.'

Now, passing the prison gate, he recalls
the young city inmate who knew by heart
'Elegy in a Country Churchyard'.

He tries to remember a line
he once thought beautiful, almost divine,
but it leaves him floundering, groping alone.

He needs to lose some weight.
Loses memory instead,
names of friends, living and dead.

Now he hears, 'Certain things must never be said.
Some secrets lie under the campanile.
Others have gone abroad.'

He thinks of names so prominent once.
Forgotten.
There's a certain comfort in oblivion.

Now, poised between right pride and shame,
he asks the dark if he was faithful
to that youthful dream.

He sees how dreams can trample dreams.
He stoops, helps one to its feet again
and shuffles with it down a tempting lane.

He wonders how much space a dream needs
to grow into its promised self.
Will the harvest pay tribute to the seeds?

He sees a face in which the dream has died
and listens as the face speaks of
the Stock Exchange and suicide.

She was born, she says, the day Martin Luther King
was shot. She quotes him now, words fiery and wise.
Do the words, or King himself, live in her eyes?

He sees a face that absurdly reminds
him of his father. Through many streets he follows
the face of an unapproachable stranger.

He sees his own face fifty years ago.
He winks at it. It winks back. There's a dance
in Bally Bee tonight. Right y'are. Let's go.

'Now is all you have,' she said.
'So go to bed and cover your head
and don't get up till Monday.'

She names two sources of sick human plight:
intimacy that rejects solitude
and the conviction that 'I'm always right'.

The mother says to the girl at the window,
'Stay there, don't move away, keep looking out.
Do you think somebody thinks you're worth looking at?'

'When they said I was mad, I began to behave
in ways they approved of.
I started with a shave.'

'My madness is what you fear
to encounter in yourself.
The magic of madness is always too near.'

He must face a face that hatred lives in
and is in love with. Hatred in love?
A post-modern myth.

'My aim always,' she insists, 'was to stay on track.
I never hated any man enough
to give him his money back.'

The old actor is speaking of his voice:
'A man should listen deeply to it.
Sometimes, it reveals his heart.'

Now to his surprise,
visited by stabwords spoken in calm rage,
he asks forgiveness of the skies.

Now a fellow passenger says, 'Forty years ago
I told you lies. You listened, looked at me, waited,
said 'All right'. I've often wondered, did you know?'

Now, Tinker, now go for it now, but you won't, will you?
You'd rather stand, stare, ponder, waver
in the grip of possibilities.

Now he dreams he backs her against the wall,
speaks his mind. She's amused, and says
'Are you Adam before, or after, the Fall?'

Now all he can say is 'O Jesus'
over and over. What's he on about?
O Jesus will we ever find out?

The man passionately talking to himself
in Warrington Place says, 'Is it any wonder
decent people won't look you in the face?'

The man spreadeagled in the doorway
of the locked pharmacy continues to plead,
'Please give me something for this pain in my head.'

He wonders if the most silent poet
on the island may be the best, but stays apart.
Not a word from him, especially about his art.

She tells how looking at the moon helped her become
an independent woman because every night, visible
or invisible, the moon slides into its kingdom.

Now the pains ambush Professor Strong.
'Old age,' he mutters, 'is such a punishment
for being young.'

The surgeon says, 'You're all right, you'll
pull through. If you only knew
the things I see every day.'

Her voice half-sings, 'He was a big, strong, violent man,
enraged, a knife in his hand.
But thank heaven for the hammer in mine!'

Approaching the Midsummer Ball,
ardent lovers practise in a bushy place.
Vigilant cherry trees know it all.

He wraps a blank page round an empty mind,
rises, opens a post-midnight window,
drinks a chilly April wind.

In darkness, lost voices live again,
accusing, loving, judging, praising, blaming.
This is the strangest kind of dreaming.

The pigeons kiss on the window-sill
and for the third time in two weeks
radio tells of a gangland killing.

Now he sees grim clouds
squabbling with each other
at the feet of the gods.

He squashes seventy years into a fistful of sand,
flings the sand into the air
and hears the laughter of the wind.

He hears a journalist twisting a story
out of Moll Brady's pain. Some folk
make a living out of mockery.

If news is the first rough draft of history
and journalism is literature in a hurry
it's important to keep reading between the lies.

Now the astronomer spills the beans
about the old universe. Billions and billions of years.
Tinker looks at the children in Moore Street.

She asks, 'Will this place ever escape
its smiling capacity for spikey gossip?
Why does it make me think of rape?'

She says, 'Sometimes, when I see the gowns,
I'm back, breathless, at Duffy's Circus,
marvelling at the clowns.'

Cars, trucks, lorries, vans roar past
the woman trying to reach her door:
'You can't be sure of your life here any more.'

Zachary Hoakes smiles, 'I'm going to spread
that rumour about her. Pure fun, of course.
Nothing to worry about in bed.'

She confides, 'This may not be discreet,
but the shrewdest creatures in Dublin
are the dogs in the street.'

He stoned a dog once.
It ran off
and was killed on the Strand Road.

He hears the travelling woman say:
'Let not your heart be troubled.
Choose the laughin' way.'

Now a voice in his battered head:
'From the depths of your mind, from the core of your blood,
write as if you were dead.'

Having cleaned the Gentlemen's Toilet
she smiles and says, 'Thanks be to God
I have the health to do it.'

They discuss some student problems:
mental illness, binge drinking, drugs, unsafe sex.
'Ah, sure we all did it, for heaven's sake!'

The German student says, 'The biggest problem
the Irish have is that they know nothing
of drinking, drugging, loving, or the meaning of fun.'

Now she asks him, 'Why do we drink like that?'
The philosophical Sophister replies, 'So that we may
forget each other.'

The moneyhunger in the fat man's voice
devours every stone of every Bank
in and out of sight.

Now he knows he doesn't understand
and is not understood.
One is the meaning of multitude.

His mind is backed against a wall.
He asks his mind, 'Have we learned
anything at all?'

The old poet advises the young writer:
'If possible, make sure you turn
your suffering into royalties!'

He observes that sometimes in summer leaves fall
as in autumn, whether on a swan's nest
or a body in the canal.

A crowd is shouting in the night.
One crowd. One shout. One night. Later,
silence prowls like the black, pattering cat.

Now he waits, is content to wait.
Decades come and go. He sees
the bodies of three robins frozen in snow.

He thinks of sweet, impotent kisses,
legs wrapped around legs, caresses
of which even silence is jealous.

He hears the old teacher swear
that the nose is the organ in which
stupidity is most readily displayed.

He admires the honesty of her cries
gleeful rejection of despair
the shining ferocity in her eyes.

The callous scribbler looks at her and says
'You look so thin, you must have cancer.'
She smiles, doesn't answer.

Moonmagic transfigures the old stones.
Great changes are happening.
The old stones are whispering.

Exam weather. Questions asked. Answers given.
She sweats. This mad weather will pass, Matilda.
Summer could be heaven.

She advises, 'If you would hear a philosopher,
show yourself fit to listen.
You will find how you move him to speak.'

'The purpose of cobbles,' said the old philosopher,
'is to distinguish between ladies and women.
Ladies never slip, even on ice.'

She holds that man is an animal fond
of contemplation. Then why do so many work so hard
being runaway slaves?

Now rheumatic Professor Tinker stares at the cranes
creating New Dublin. Walking, he counts forty-three.
He is an ancient mariner longing for coffee.

Why, after decades of study and living by rule
does the pleasant, humane old scholar
feel such a fool?

She smells herself; flesh, perhaps bone,
and is quick to admit she enjoys
smelling alone.

He smells her all over
with such loving skill she wishes
the night would be forever.

'If you could be a flower,' he says,
'which would you choose to be?'
She smiles, 'Which flower would choose to be me?'

It happened thirty years ago
yet when they pass each other in Leeson Street
she smells the hatred through his eyes.

She still thinks the best lectures
she ever heard were given by a man
who spoke as though he stood on a dunghill.

Hearing about his gossip of her faults, she says,
'He knows nothing of my other faults. If he did,
he wouldn't limit himself to these.'

She smiles through a tale of old horrors
and says that she drinks
for fun and through sorrows.

The grey-backed crow is owner of the field.
Like Professor Hoggett and his theories
he'll never yield.

Professor Hoggett thinks of love. His theory about that?
Love is the steam rising
from the boiling kettle of hate.

Her song at the century's turning
begins with, 'We're no more poisonous
than your average Centre of Learning.'

He's quick to admit he's a loser-lover
though his heart is stitched with memories.
Sometimes, now is forever.

Now the philosopher: 'There is no difference between living
and dying.' 'Why, then, do you not die?'
'Because there is no difference.'

She halts, wonders how a city changes
like a friendship or a marriage
or the leaf at her feet, crinkled with age.

She studies history passionately and yet
lies awake at night thinking of what
she'd love to forget.

He's grateful for the fertile skies
frost outside the window
her hot paradise thighs.

He cries
and doesn't know why
hope floods his eyes.

Sometimes, eyes are sharp teeth
chewing what they look at.
And they know what to spit out.

The wicked wind turns branches into Vikings
striking the sea again,
merciless, skilled, conquering men.

Board Meeting minutes hammered her head.
Asked what she thought of the old place now
'This is a hard hat site,' she said.

He meets a woman who's a hundred and three.
'Congrats,' he says, 'how did you reach that age?'
'Don't worry,' she says. 'Don't worry.'

The young motorist hoots in rage
at the old man stickshuffling across the road.
Unacceptable! Youth stalled by old age!

She asks the painter why, since he makes such beautiful
things, his children are so ugly. The painter says
he makes paintings by day, children by night.

'That man, like a hare, is always in a state of fright.
Leaves falling from trees in autumn
are enough to put him to flight.'

Although partridges steal eggs from each other,
the young born of these eggs
always return to their true mother.

'Such a night of dreams!
But now, every dream is gone from me
and the cheeky Liffey is laughing at the sea!'

The tired man pleads, 'Please do not reveal,
if freedom is precious to you,
that my face is the prison of love.'

'It's the weekend that gets 'em,' he said,
referring to lonely academics. Weeks later,
his wife bolted to Spain with a lonely philosopher.

Einstein's eyes have floated in a small glass jar
in a New Jersey safe-deposit box
for nearly fifty years.

Cissy wants to interview Einstein
but stumbling on him in the nude leads her
to write a brilliant non-interview for a famous paper.

'He is,' she says, 'a man who says exactly what he feels:
'World peace is possible
with proper organisation and the right ideals.'

When she looks at him like that, he sees her eyes
are steadfast stars that he may wonder at
but never know.

He thinks it might be easier to find
names for stars than words
for the workings of her eyes.

Not for the first time he hears the talking bone:
'Let not your rage or hate destroy a life;
if you don't value it, you don't deserve your own.'

It's the kind of day when she can hardly muster
sufficient interest to witness blue turning sickly grey
or purple robbing red of its lustre.

Kitty had never met him, but her tongue meets everyone.
'Be careful there,' she advises Elizabeth,
'they tell me he's a womaniser.'

She draws a line down the middle of the bed
and stretches on it. 'What can I do?' he asks.
'Toe the line,' she says.

She'll conquer him yet
with a style he'll never escape or forget
because the woman is at home in her own sweat.

Gossip flows through the place like the Liffey
and some of the most venomous gossips
are practised bum-waddlers, posh and sniffy.

'Gossip keeps the Irish alive,' says Angela Drew.
'When the Chinese take over the island
we'll turn them into gossips too.'

Professor Tinker is a quiet man,
perhaps the original quiet man,
so quiet, he attracts attention.

Quietness of the mind sometimes enables a mind
to read other minds. For Tinker, this is one
of the rewards for hosting darkness.

He looks straight in the gossip's face,
a beautiful, vicious creation
at home in a beautiful place.

In his retirement speech, Professor Hooke
said he'd rather read a colleague
than his book.

How did Hooke live to a hundred and three?
The occasional trip to Ardee
and Olympian doses of Vitamin C.

Hooke says growing old is an art
we ought to study more.
Lesson one: How not to be a bore.

'There are three ages of man,' says Penelope Dell:
'youth, middle age,
and you're lookin' well.'

'I cherish my enemies,' Tinker said.
'Their views of me are nearer the truth
than how I see myself.'

Go through today without a pill.
See pigeons on the window-sill.
Love to eat. Beak well. Not slow to kill.

'The art of the twentieth century's most
profound playwright boils down to this:
he knew how to take the piss.'

Sneering is an art
perfected by a few.
When all else fails, a well-timed sneer may do.

'You chose the scenic route', he said.
'I went the private road.'
Is that why he thinks he's God?

'Every man came out of a woman,' says Leo Flynn.
'Is it any wonder he spends the rest of his life
tryin' to get back in?'

Did the man who split the atom
foresee what we
can hardly say?

'If, on the morning of my wedding day,
I got the briefest glimpse of the future,
the entire party would still be waiting.'

'You can download love,' she said,
'and be uplifted
but spot the gossips who'd see you shafted.'

After heavy rain, he sees faces in clouds.
They're born, grow into themselves, replace each other:
James Joyce, Jesus Christ, his dead brother.

There is no now and there is nothing but now.
Listen to the clock.
Love's pulse goes tick-tock.

Her sweating wrist softens the strap.
Now she knows he'll never flop across her
or she play Chinese tricks on his lap.

She sings a song of pain and wonder
that comforts other folk
but deepens pain within her.

The most cheerful woman he has met for a long while
chops corpses for a living.
Her mind, especially, has a winning smile.

Tinker knows Hogge well:
an ego beyond all measurement
and impenetrable.

She's gone,
leaving him with castrating pain.
Young clouds can bring old rain.

The bitter moment passes.
A woman strides with yellow flowers
so quickly, they could be roses.

Some sixty years with Plato and his breed
cannot help him to forget
smiling Annie Creed.

Butt Bridge. Sunny. Never saw her before,
woman in blue dress, yellow hat.
'Oho,' she chortles, 'I know what you're laughin' at!'

Tinker knows a man who refuses to smile
because, he says, a smile is a hypocritical
caricature of his true style.

Asked why he prefers PlayStation to Leggo
seven-year-old Will smiles and says
'I love to kill.'

For forty years he's walked that street to work.
Coming home one night, he was beaten up. A jeering gang.
He'll never walk that street again.

Three teenagers beat up the eighty-year-old,
tie him up, dump him in his room, lock him in,
escape with twenty euro.

Ask the old hurler, back to the wall, about his many
scars, he'll say 'My scars are stories
the great game wrote on my body.'

Ask the old footballer why he won't stop
drinking, he'll say, 'Life off the field is dreary and dull.
On the field, I was hero, winner, fox and bull.'

How much violence hides in educated voices?
Some questions find answers like silence in the air
when the last train passes.

She tricked him into it, he tricked her
out of it, and such was the art of it
they finished back where they started.

Who can do justice to the seagull?
The smile on the sky's face
loves the beautiful unreachable.

Melanie Horne is beyond his reach.
He stands alone on a desolate beach
smelling and feeling the sea's winter touch.

For Tinker, the years are distinct colours,
blue green yellow red purple black
and whatever is the colour of the shell stuck to the rock

'I lost my sense of smell fifteen years ago.
What's my body like?
How would I know?'

To have someone shape your life, and never
to have touched her, is, fifty years later,
a fresh and grateful wonder.

He walks along Westmoreland Street.
She passes, perfumed, eloquently neat.
Dear God! When did Dublin smell so sweet?

Sunday morning: she walks over the Seán O'Casey bridge
down by the edge of the Liffey
where the air is pure and the gulls are happy.

The summerstink runs through the city now
sore eyes, sore throats, uncountable cars
and the hellsmell spreading like poisonous rumours.

'Idiots in positions of power,' she says,
'never listen to anyone, including
themselves. Listen to their babbling.'

Again the flowerman smells the flower,
draws back, leans forward, kisses it
with tenderness would please a lover.

'When you listen to him and he
listens to you, I am happy to listen
to both of you.'

The Japanese actor describes the Hiroshima smell.
His eyes are pearls
at the bottom of the sea.

The strangest smell is the smell of hatred in the air
between two people who once were friends.
It's deeper than the sea and knows no bounds.

When she describes him now, she is describing
the smell of wrong. She banished that,
and hopes to live free and long.

Does she smell herself to see if her mind
will tell her she's irresistible or unbearable?
Smell yourself and tell the air what you find.

'There's one perfume I love. It sets me free.
Let nobody ever ask me to change it.
It's my smell, the smell I am, and will always be.'

'Smell me,' she whispers, 'I'm like a mackerel
or maybe the salmon of knowledge.
Smell me. You'll have a story to tell.'

When the foulness of traffic
meets the sweetness of woman
Tinker knows what matters.

The economist sneers at the poem.
The poem smiles back at him.
The economist can't begin to analyse the smile.

The economist knows he knows it all.
He has a suit, a shirt, a tie, a bag, dead words.
He can't begin to sniff the death he exhales.

The economist dons his prophet's hat.
'On the one hand... On the other hand...'
O smell the mud on Sandymount strand.

'The old man was kicked and maimed by drunken vandals.
We'll be back after the break
with the Health scandals.'

'Don't just sit there, waiting to die.
Look at the sky. You'd never know when you
might find a new, surprising way to fly.'

She was broke for far too long.
Now she makes a thousand a night
thanks to Dublin and Hong Kong.

'Rationalism is fear of imaginative potential,'
she laughs as she opens her mind
and her legs to Jaymoney Bastible.

Tinker listens to the talk of planners
and it strikes him now, in his eightieth year,
that stars and words are his favourite dancers.

Things could turn out fine
if politicians learn to follow
Bono's melody line.

Whenever he says a prayer
his toes tap happily on the floor
because God has a musical ear.

Listen to Bono now, his words, his music
satisfying a deep-as-history need.
Can music save the world from greed?

One of her eyes is blue, the other brown.
Late on certain nights, however, she says
both are green.

Two magpies croak and circle each other.
Of almost any two creatures, why does one
nearly always seem to want to make love?

Eyes are the heart's ambassadors
but sometimes they change policies
in mid-conversation.

Children play at the sea's edge,
waves break in homage
at their wild delight.

Tinker stares at the sea,
asking the question he has always asked:
what are you saying to me?

Now, Tinker senses the sea's rage
fuming to change into a sea of blood
choosing its moment to explode.

Sprawled in summer grass,
legs twined, is either lover dreaming
of what may never come to pass?

Breasts are flowers, no doubt about that.
Barney Anvil says they're chocolate
at heaven's gate.

When she flicks her eyes
in the middle of a conversation
she solves and creates mysteries.

Whoever looks in her eyes
will find countries
not found in maps.

Her eyes light up, look down, then sideways,
all in a flash. She sees more in that moment
than he has seen in years.

He almost drowned twice.
Once in the Shannon,
once in her eyes.

The postcard means little to him.
When she reads it, however,
her mouth is laughing but her eyes are grim.

There are those who've never clapped eyes
on each other
and yet are sisters and brothers.

He looks the killer in the eyes
and understands why people say
it's better not to. Look straight ahead.

When does innocence die in eyes?
Why is so much style a lie?
Why is fake laughter a sad story?

Now she sees him as never before.
Her eyes enjoy new life in her, in him
who was once a stranger knocking at her door.

'All men naturally desire to know.'
How many desire to see?
Father, brother, please turn your eyes on me.

When he and she were both nine years of age
she looked at him one day. Whatever lived
in her eyes then made him her estranged love forever.

Now her eyes are a tribunal.
Like poetry, she is a court
of judgement on the soul.

Do eyes think?
Do they publish quietly?
Who has not read a story in a blink?

Her eyes cut through his eyes, down into his heart,
explore it with a relaxed ferocity
some creators say is the heart of art.

She heard it first at the corner of a bridge,
pure music of water. She forgot it for years
but heard it again when sickness damaged her eyes and ears.

Secretly he tries to count her words.
If each word was a step, she'd reach heaven
in no time. No time. No words. Heaven. Over to you, words.

When illness became waiting for death
she summoned from her heart the music she loved most
as though preparing to become a happy ghost.

Everyone else is eager to know what Beethoven heard.
When the boy falls from the top of Mount Brandon
his cry inhabits an abandoned island.

I would love to know if you hear what I hear.
Do words amount to a large whiskey
or a modest glass of beer?

The voice she hears now will not be the same
as the video voice in ten years time.
In disbelief, she'll beg forgiveness of a name.

When words make love to each other
some beautiful children are born
and the occasional monster.

Where do nightwords go during the day?
Can light begin to understand
what darkness has to say?

There is a darkness that almost crushes the mind
but then withdraws a little, has mercy, and allows
the black dog to hunt in other places.

Brendan Behan was terrified of darkness,
always slept with the light on.
He learned this in prison.

Now the lovers listen to each other.
They listen. What do they hear?
A year together will provide an answer.

Now the drum beats its rhythm of rage.
Fifteen policemen are injured.
Aspiring killers take to the stage.

Trees swallow the brash sounds of men
with such cool dignity I see why
we once dreamed our world was a garden.

Are there more mad noises in the head
than in the world outside?
His eyes close. What dreambombs will explode?

When the soul is starved, gossip is a slice
of fresh bread. Chew. Swallow. Digest. Excrete.
Tomorrow may bring some beautifully butchered meat.

The first time she heard of Snow White
she counted to seven. That evening
was the door to mathematics and magic.

'I often ask myself,' the scholar said, 'why do I need
to dig for years in order to write a book
that few, or maybe none, will read?'

Now he listens to the old policeman:
'Forty years ago, murders in Ireland were rare.
Now they happen nearly every day.'

Do murder and money go hand in hand?
Is murder an inevitable aspect of "progress"?
Or was it all just waiting to happen in Ireland?

Does education produce polished, callous bastards
who know how to smile, and where, and when,
until they seem esteemed by other men?

I've said it before, let me say it again.
One well-timed look in his eyes
will tell you more than a dozen biographies.

Now he is learning to relax,
picking moments from the years
like a lad picking periwinkles from rocks.

Yesterday that line warmed the page.
Now it's a bird with one wing
and so he works to help it sing.

'Everyone can sing,' the woman said, 'but they don't know
or won't admit the beauty of their voices.
Believe, I say, believe. And let your magic flow.'

'Don't ask me why I think of you, dear man,
whenever I flip a fresh cod
in my old, reliable frying pan.'

'I loving you, you not loving me,
by your power and my consent
we conquered me.'

Now she sees a look in his eyes
that makes her turn aside and then
resolve never to see him again.

Some are afraid to love, some are afraid to sing,
some are afraid to say how fear
becomes the dominant, shaping, tyrant thing.

If we all knew what each one
says of the other would there be
six friends left in the world?

'I believe,' she said, 'he would use a hatchet
to remove a fly
from my forehead.'

He finds the book thirty years after he got it.
All night, he sits and reads it.
Now he'll never lose it.

Now she hears a voice from long ago:
'When poverty walks in the door
love flies out the window.'

In a time outside time, she is being used
in a way she can scarcely imagine:
a small man, coarse, from the top of Sweden.

The tree is so peaceful, tall and strong
Tinker looks at it for hours,
admiring, loving, grateful, wondering.

Perhaps, in mid-winter, the trees, stripped
naked now like women in men's minds,
bend and confide in each other.

Scrawled on a Camden Street wall:
In a time of ugliness
protest is beautiful.

After a month, the young gay man is conscious again,
his attacker's words still ringing in his ears:
'Great fun, kickin' the shit outa fuckin' queers!'

Now the trees stand still and attentive as monks
heads bowed before an altar of darkness
and whatever waits to happen.

'Tell me this,' she says, 'have you dared to live?'
He stands, wordless. Never before has anyone
asked him this. And probably never again.

The system advises him he must learn how to smile
and stop slouching like the Hunchback of Notre Dame.
Think, the system says. Next year may be The Grand Slam.

'Why do I always put off till tomorrow what I
should do today?' he asks himself. 'Why
am I so afraid of now?'

He sneezes on the clifftop
and says 'Excuse me'
although the nearest human is miles away.

Now, strolling with her husband, she meets
and greets a man she might have married.
Her smiles back, walks on, a little hurried.

'Now we're into the new century,' Myles Butterman says,
'and, be it blessing or curse,
our self-deception is getting worse. Well, mine is.'

How long before a poisoned world
stumbles and falls on the flat of its back,
dead to the Zodiac?

The words we throw away
outnumber the enchanting stars
shining on peace and war.

In this city of rumours, malice flows
like the fabled, wrinkled Liffey.
God alone knows where it goes.

'He makes millions every year,' whispers Zachary Raine,
'but the wife is cuttin' loose
and he's havin' trouble with cocaine.'

Tinker is at home only when he's lost
in thought or what seems like thought.
He laughs at himself then for being both jockey and horse.

'In this futuristic place,' says Angela Barlow
'there are moments I ask myself and you,
are we ditching humanity?'

Hear now the wise words of the analyst:
'If you can't pay your way
you have no right to exist.'

'I like him,' she says, 'he's bisexual,
a delightful mixture
of desire and fear.'

Another Chinese man was stabbed to death last night
by a youngster who stole his car.
The youngster escaped. The car was found, burnt out.

Many young men now, impeccably dressed
and slaving hard at the business of staying alive,
are burnt out by the time they're thirty-five.

People will get used to anything
The sense of shock is short-lived.
Blood-donors are getting scarce.

She's tired and hungry, depressed and pale.
She says, 'The most important thing in life for me
is to create something beautiful.'

Now. Know. No k. OK?
Words are strong old houses
and every word is its own lock and key.

When he was ten
his mind was locked by a cruel teacher.
Forty years on, will it ever open again?

Men who cut themselves off from the mystery of words
wear practised smiles on their faces
and have hammers in their heads.

There is a summer stillness no words can capture,
so let it be. Language moves away
to the corner of another day.

Words, like good neighbours, borrow from each other,
helping each other live in story and song,
trying to get it right, aware of the ways of wrong.

All we know is stories about each other, muses
Tinker, thinking of colleagues, their special words,
their favourite thoughts, their working faces.

'She was a good teacher,' the ex-student said.
'I remember her as if she were a song.
She brought such joy to the young.'

Tinker's loneliness makes him a good listener.
Now he listens to voices in his mind
and outside, a belligerent summer wind.

Every sound he hears at night is a longing
for connection. Darkness is a stage waiting
for players to greet the singing light.

'Yes, I have lived. No, I'm not afraid to go mad.
Twenty years in Africa freed my head.
Bono is a saint,' she said.

'Freedom of the city is not enough for a man
like that. He deserves the freedom
of at least one universe.'

Bored with her men
she married her computer
and discovered conversation.

She walks away from him now
perfecting the Eden rhythm of her buttocks.
And Adam me boy, does she know how!

He flings his folly out the window.
It falls like shredded theology
into the arms of Information Technology.

Now the epic self-deception of experts sees now
as the only time that ever existed.
It's time for a year in Stratford.

'I did two years in Mountjoy,' says Knuckle Canty,
'and I learned to lead a life
of quiet ecstasy.'

Avoiding the countless expensive cars
a horse goes galloping happily
through the streets of Dublin.

'Looking forward, it seemed like eternity.
Looking back now, it's a moment.
I'll settle for now.'

'She's gone to hospital to have her baby.
He's gone off to play golf.
A happy couple.'

She says she's having an operation
next week
to remove her tongue from her cheek.

'Stop! Don't try to fool me,' barks Professor Wyse.
'Now is now. Now is not then, it's only a version of then.
Much history is bloody lies!'

Now another could-be killer in a car
barely misses a pedestrian.
He opens his window and shouts 'Fuck off!'

Who knows how behind-the-wheel rage
turns a mild man in a silver car
into a cursing savage?

Look at his face now,
that man like a well-dressed rat.
Curses are stronger when they're spat.

Now the smokers gather outside the office
in the rain.
For a moist moment, they're happy again.

Witnessing the starry midnight sky
Tinker knows true privilege
despite the pain cracking his back.

Blue white grey black O changing sky,
why, looking at you now, does Tinker
think of love, this truth, that lie?

They both know her story yet neither
tells it, or will begin to tell it.
Silence keeps many a marriage together.

The poem smiled at her, took her by the hand,
walked with her down the street of pain.
She felt better then.

All night long, three lights on the huge crane
flash in warning, it must be warning
as Tinker scans the sky for signs of morning.

'Whether in business, science, politics or the arts,
some men,' says Simona James, 'simply theorise
passion out of their hearts.'

Tinker looks at flowers this evening.
No passionate flowerman he, and yet
God's tears through black railings he'll not forget.

Hooke likes the system. He works for it. It works for him.
They're very close. It's a deepening relationship.
Maybe one day they'll get married.

He married the system for several years
but got divorced when the system
had an affair with Pat Masters.

Sometimes, thinks Tinker, I think the system is a slut.
But what man doesn't love a slut?
Male, female or e-mail, we love a slut.

What she said to him on the bridge after they'd dined
together that evening will live longer in his mind
and heart than the taste of his favourite German wine.

How is it that moments from fifty years ago
are more living now than they were then?
The hammer missed his brother's head. Amen.

How come atrocities may be forgotten
but one stabbing remark
will haunt the heart forever?

Tinker is angry now. Can't talk to anyone. Must be alone.
Starts walking. Anywhere. Finds a shabby old seat,
sits, stares at the Liffey. Eyes of fire. Man of stone.

The old man sick in the bed is a tyrant.
He can turn even sickness into a weapon.
Only one woman dares whisper, 'Beware of his pain!'

'Don't ask me,' he said, 'answers don't come easy to me
but the more I see of education
the more I gawp at polished dishonesty.'

'Education is business,' Professor Keane said.
'Forget about the majestic dead.
Money demands we always look ahead.'

'What do you make of it now?' queries Lance Magee.
'Six days of the week I'm a slave.
One day, I'm weary and nearly free.'

'Tell me a line
You'll remember all your life.'
'If I were human enough I might recognise the divine.'

Now relieved of fire and stone, he prays God
to let his mind be strong enough to face
the days ahead; let anger talk to grace.

'The good go first,' she said,
remembering how her father and brother
drowned.

Foresight and Hindsight meet in a Dublin pub.
Hindsight remarks, 'You're lookin' well.'
Foresight replies, 'Something you said helped me to sidestep hell.'

Is the old footballer talking to himself?
'Hit the enemy hard and square
but never boot a man when he's down.'

'She's the rose, he's the thorn.
All who fight for birth control
have already been born.'

Now, in business, the tap-on-the-shoulder technique
works well. Hunt's shoulder was tapped yesterday.
Today, he's broke.

Simon Clear learned the hard way.
First, he survived poverty.
Later, he survived money.'

Picasso dug his way through philosophy
and concluded he'd like to live like a poor man
with plenty money.

Is there a madder creature on God's once green earth
than this motorbike maniac in Pearse Street
bullyroaring his way to somewhere?

When Tinker reads 'The Word was made flesh'
he dreams there's a right proverb
for every man and woman.

'A light heart lives long,' she laughs.
'Never let the bastards get you down.
A day in the country is worth a month in the town.'

If it's true that where there's muck there's money
it's also true that a rambling bee
brings home the honey.

The old footballer touches his spine:
'Amazing what a quick kick in the back can do.
Forty years ago, one moment in that field changed my life.'

'My husband and I love to gossip because
it shows a healthy interest in our neighbours,
as healthy, indeed, as their interest in our affairs.'

No stopping this gossipy man.
The dirt that comes out of a hole
will fill it up again.

'Such a kind man, but talks non-stop about sex.
He's like a story that cannot be told.'
Then he says, 'I'm growing old.'

'Academic gossip is quite delightful,
clever bites from the well-dressed,
some savage titbits from the depressed.'

After forty years strolling through Manhattan
she returns to Dublin
to press the green button.

The scientist is getting hysterical: the energy
that makes the tides rise and fall must be captured
or we lose money.

He says money will do anything.
She says it's likely
he'll do anything for money.

She says money animates a tired soul,
cleans a filthy body
and makes an old man a bridegroom.

The old terrorist learned from what he chose to do:
a loaded gun terrifies one person,
an unloaded gun terrifies two.

Morning light
can sometimes heal
the mad sickness of night.

Why is darkness so riddled with guilt?
Why do years become hammers
in the hands of demons?

She has such power when she talks like that.
When she changes her style
she's an empty matchbox.

'The people I love most,' says Granny Arden,
'are those who live and love the moment
and don't blame now for not being then.'

Klone dreams of visiting Chekhov's birthplace.
He dreams of perfecting his secret art.
He spends much of his life squatting in the Dart.

She enthuses, 'Writing, is it? Another day, another dollar.
Emily wrote well without a man.
Joyce was a Jesuit without a collar.'

'A poem should not mean
but be.'
'On the matter of meaning and being, we disagree.'

Words use people more than people use words.
When Tinker found this, he became
a silent island, a long winter.

He walks along the edges of himself,
listening to the sea
scattering gifts and warnings tirelessly.

He bends and picks a shell, presses it
to his ear. O the magical sound
he's privileged to hear!

The swan cocks his arse
to the full moon,
going down.

Tinker had a dream,
still has. That's why he's determined
not to marry the system.

How much of a man is lost in success?
Quite a lot she thinks, looking at the man
to whom she almost said yes.

Certain midnight creatures shine in darkness.
Nameless they never vanish but gift their magic,
flying in and out of lonely eyes.

Some old eyes retain an innocence
after eighty years.
Now riddle me that, me Trinity scholar.

Words trawl the darkness now
picking secrets out of the deep, secrets
like a bundle of yesterdays wrapped in a black ribbon.

'You're ninety-eight! What keeps you alive, Red Hugh?'
'My heart! My spirit! My heart! And tellin'
Bare-faced lies to the likes o' you!'

This old man longs to be bellicose
but must settle for a scrap
with the hair growing out of his nose.

'Hope's words are worth repeating, for love's sweet sake:
You know you're getting old
when the candles cost more than the cake.'

'Yes,' he says, 'I'm a mean man, and I thought
I'd grow meaner with age. But now that I'm old
I'm happy to give most things away.'

'Mean!' she explodes, 'he'd steal the eye
out of your head and then come back
for the other one!'

'What I hate most,' he says, 'is being offered a seat
on a bus by a beautiful young woman
who once, in an instant, would've set me in heat!'

'Now, what I need most,' he says, 'is a wise
irrefutable Oriental proverb to lie at my side
and gentle me to sleep.'

No sleep tonight, so he sits alone in the dark
which offers, in its own good time,
the music of silence.

Murders, drugs, corruption,
progress.
But Molly still says yes.

He can hardly believe it. After days
and nights without speaking, one morning,
shyly, he says the right thing.

Now they make love between two apple trees.
His eyes are closed. In summer evening light
she sees an apple she'd love to bite.

It takes a tricky light to turn a treetop
into a gaunt Caesar assessing rises and falls
after the day's Stock Exchange battles.

He brags of length and size.
She turns from the window,
photographs him with her eyes.

He thinks he's getting away with it now
but the poor lad has forgotten
the eyes at the back of her head.

No bragging now.
He was flooded out of his house last night.
Summer. A place to stay?

He worships the ground
she walks on and is glad to find
her father owns the land.

Her eyes follow him everywhere.
They witness his every move
even when she's not there.

The quiet ferocity of the rhythm
that dictates his life strikes him now
like a stone of understanding hitting his head.

Midnight. They squat in a corner of the cricket pitch,
meditating. Traffic, never resting, crashes past.
The moon has a thoughtful look.

Eileen Collins is back from space
with a look of original wonder
on her strong, life-loving, celebrating face.

'Shelter me,' she pleads. 'They say I'm mad.
I know I'm not.'
'That's the best shelter you've got.'

Why, when you give them
what they ask for,
do they ask for more and more?

Black suit. Black bag. Eternal mobile phone.
What is a happy moment?
Alone.

'Yes, of course I repeat myself. Who listens
to what you or I have to say?
Do you remember three sentences you spoke today?'

He tries to write, precisely as he can,
things his father said. He wonders now
if his father was a talkative man.

When he proposed to her, what did he say?
It's forty years on, but you'd think he might recall
what words prompted her to hop off the wall.

Strong words become echoes, echoes become wings
feathering their way through heart and brain
until strong words are born again.

'Turn me loose,' she says 'or turn me up or down
or in or out, but turn me on.
It's time for a marathon.'

He's drunk, drugged, foul-mouthed, self-obsessed,
resolutely grim.
She's calm and beautiful and she kisses him.

Is Art useless?
Will Science destroy the world?
Can Molly McGrath afford a new bicycle?

Tinker's body and mind turn their backs on sleep.
It's a long battle between dark and light.
Is that why he learns something every night?

The most terrifying thing about learning
is that it must lead to silence.
But listen! Someone in West Cork is starting to talk:

Talk to him. He seems to listen. He smiles.
He nods his seeminglistening head. He smiles.
He seems to take it all in. You wonder. He smiles.

'If I don't get out of here,' she says, 'I'll go mad.
A fortnight in Majorca, a week in Paris
and a week in London might make Dublin bearable.'

She can hardly bear the sight of him now.
And to think they once explored Australia together
loving it, and each other, every step of the way.

At what moment will she decide to go?
She'll watch him munching-crunching Corn Flakes one morning,
three words like music in her head, 'Now I know.'

The capacity of true lovers to vanish
out of each other's lives is celebrated this morning
by a blackbird on a solitary bush.

'I don't know why I write to you.
You never reply.
Give it a chance to live before you let it die.'

'I want one thing only.
You in me.
Why do you look like a frightened bee?'

'Ravenous appetite my arse!
A man is no more
than a lusty goat waiting to snore!'

Another sleepless night for Tinker.
If he could sleep and choose his dream
he'd witness the birth of his father and mother.

Dreams cannot be chosen.
They visit us, mostly in bed.
Are you ready?

'Marry me,' she says. 'You have until Saturday night
to make up your mind.' He's worried now:
'Will her beauty crush my genius?'

'Never say *fall*
in love again.
Soar in love from now on.'

'Talk to yourself,' my father said,
'and you'll know what to do.'
I talked to myself. Now, let me sing for you.

'Why are you always talking to yourself?'
the Inspector asks Patricia Flood.
'Because the company is good.'

He went insane because he couldn't stop
thinking. His great gift drove him mad.
That's what they said. That's what they repeated.

It is not widely known
that jesting Pilate, famous for his jokes,
became Rome's most celebrated clown.

Say something. Write it. Print it. Make it stick.
You can make him into someone he never was
or will be. Print can be arsenic.

'Too many words', she sang. 'Gaza. Strip.
Chop the land. Smash the rocks. Find
the diamond.'

One murder was committed here in 1954.
Now, five murders in ten days.
Progress.

Headlines last a day, or part of a day.
Atrocities at breakfast are forgotten at lunch.
Horror piled on horror melts away.

She knows no one is there.
Yet if she stares and stares
she'll see that face somewhere.

'Don't get me wrong, though some say I'm sick.
My dislike of that woman
is purely platonic.'

He reads the anonymous letter.
It dubs him a mind-fucker.
How can he answer?

Not everybody is as hurtful as nobody
when nobody, out of his no-life,
chooses his special knife.

He once asked Eily Kilbride
who was her favourite poet.
'Anon,' she replied.

When hate's arteries begin to harden
she likes to stroll, not in her own
but in her neighbour's garden.

What she likes about hate is the cold
perspective it gives her on herself
and on what decent folk call the world.

Hatred learned in childhood has lasted
his lifetime, sustaining him through trouble and pain.
'Hatred is precious,' he says. 'Not a shred should be wasted.'

'He's some storyteller,' she says,
'the only man I know who, with
a deft flick of his madness, can mythologise myth.'

Suppose not a word is lost.
Every word has been recorded
and is known to every ghost.

Tinker asks the theologian, 'What is a lie?'
'I don't know,' he says, 'but I continue
to ask the question of the sea at high tide.'

The sea has a ring of truth
in stillness and in storm,
in pure peace and raging harm.

Enraged drivers of flashy cars never lie.
They just curse anyone
who gets in their way.

The furious, foul impatience
no other soul can truly feel
drives the man behind the wheel.

Rage is a horn, blasting
the newborn infant's tear
early in the morning.

'If I could always speak the truth
I think I would live
with a shut mouth.'

Can you name what is lurking at the back
of your mind? If you could slit your brain
would it fly out like a swallow?

'I think I could learn to cherish
this place if I were a swallow:
visit for a few warm weeks, then vanish.'

Living with the bullishly familiar can be
quite a task, but growing to see it truly
is a joy.

Three ducks drift in the canal,
relaxed as diplomats on holidays
until a woman throws bread in the water.

No, I'm not going to force it to end.
That would be like forcing a friend
to be a friend.

She travels in a land beyond reason,
a land flourishing beyond the real
because of a passing smile.

All night Tinker sits and thinks of friends.
So many he believed he knew.
Now, so few.

'O kiss me arse,' she chirps, 'forget your gloomy style.
It takes forty-two muscles to frown,
seventeen to smile.'

When she told him her elder sister had died
he smiled.
To this day, she often wonders why.

The old footballer remembers, 'Crowther
nearly crippled me.' He smiles. 'But then,
I nearly crippled his brother.'

He's determined to surpass his father and brother.
Self-empowerment and self-deception
can dynamise each other.

The smile on the infant's face
is so glorious
it feels like a national holiday.

Three storeys up, Tinker sees pieces of bread
pitched and scattered on the pavement:
bits of self lost in streets through his head.

Reassembling bits of self sometimes gives him
the pleasant feeling
that goes with end-of-summer harvesting.

'I never knew Saint Patrick was a British star.
'Twas him changed us from being pagans
into whatever it is we are.'

It's one thing to sweat and puke through
an airport summer
but quite another to pretend it was fun.

'How are you?' 'Grand. Couldn't be better
since I gave up chips, crisps, cream,
Guinness, chocolate and beautiful butter.'

Her lips move silently in autumn air.
Is she saying a poem? A prayer?
Or a curse on someone, somewhere?

The shy Chinese girl has the most beautiful lips
Tinker has ever seen. She works hard,
and looks directly at no one.

In prison, de Valéra learned to speak
without moving his lips.
That's when he said most.

If the lips of Judas were auctioned
in Sotheby's now
how much would they fetch?

'Even when she lies to me, her lips
are the most beautiful I've ever seen.
I could listen to her lies all night.'

The play is over, the theatre empty, the moon full.
A lying mouth
destroys the soul.

'In the case of the accomplished liar
eyes collaborate with lips.
Study both.'

She stops in the middle of Grafton Street
to rub a shine on her lips.
She moves on then, first of the Tall Ships.

When George Dawson was dying in Bloomfield
his lips moved.
I think he was talking to God.

Lips are tireless workers.
Even in sleep, they serve the creatures of dream,
obeying those with or without a name.

'My lips loved to be licked by a loving tongue.
All moist again,
hungry and young.'

Some old lips are crinkled paper
where words are difficult to read.
Is wisdom a compensation for lack of blood?

It's not that he took a vow of silence,
he simply stopped speaking,
content to listen to his life's voices.

Whenever she sits alone for a day and a night
listening to voices,
she whimpers, laughs, cowers, glows, laments, rejoices.

Every liar has his own way.
The White House has nothing to hide.
The biggest liar of all is *They Say*.

'Words don't like being used to lie.
A liar needs a good memory.
Words know the moment of revenge.'

Tinker thinks of his friend who says nothing
now. Somehow or other,
he hears him more clearly than ever.

Why do we blame time for being cruel,
muses Tinker, when it's we who are cruel to time,
most of the time?

He stands at the corner of Grafton Street,
begging, cap outstretched: 'Please, please give me
your wasted hours.'

'In Ireland now,' says Zoe Holmes
'few people own houses.
Houses own them.'

'My husband is boring me to madness,' she said.
'There was a time he laughed with Cupid.
Now all he wants is to be stuffed and stupid.'

'My image of a stupid man,' she says,
'is a glutton spreadeagled in front of a telly,
increasingly smelly.'

'Will she ever shut up?
Why can't the thoughtless
be wordless?'

'There is no braver creature on earth
than this brave woman.
She was born, and lives, to see justice done.'

Homeless people are dying
on the streets of Dublin.
Gangland killings happen often.

Now she walks across Main Square.
In forty years' time, they'll say no more
beautiful woman ever walked there.

True progress between opposites? Can this be true?
Tinker looks at the sky that seems as though
we have beaten it black and blue.

'The few poets I know,' says Hogge, 'love beauty
and are worried about how their books sell.
Where would the poor devils be without their hell?'

Who is the man looking down on the sleeping Queen?
Who is the young woman entranced by the hasbeen?
Why does Green kill Orange, Orange kill Green?

How would they survive without this hatred
of each other? It keeps them going
through threats of decency.

Tinker's knowledge of hell is alive at moments
such as now when a young woman praises
murderous violence.

The more I think of now, flicks Tinker, the less
I understand it, and the more I long
for time's caress.

There is an emptiness he'll never measure or understand.
So he sips wine, reads a book, or returns for a moment
to his favourite boyhood band.

Say now for every step you take,
every now, like every step, is in the past,
the savage, calm, insatiable past.

It's as though the world is a huge fist
made of mockery, and Tinker is a fly
tripping from knuckle to knuckle.

This woman, unfamiliar stranger, seems about to cry
but then says calmly, 'I work with men, I
keep my head down, do my best, goodbye.'

'To survive in Dublin,' advises Rolex, 'a poet needs
a deeply sensitive nature
and a neck like a jockey's bollocks.'

'There are Nazi eyes from Donegal to Dingle
but here, my dear,
you're watched from every angle.'

Two men in two boats attack the bushes
in the canal. This is an autumn war.
The bushes fight bravely but the boats will conquer.

'Help her, dear God,' he prays. 'Help her. Help her.'
A small bird on the window-sill
sings 'I will! I will! I will!'

'Bruised hands, bruised lips, bruised eyes,' she said,
'prove once again that I let my heart
rule my head.'

In all this ruck and madness, here's a moment
beyond words, still, so still.
Let it come, let it go, let it return, if it will.

He was trapped in a poem for forty years.
One morning, the poem opened a side-door.
He slipped out into a world of new wonders.

He could be a beggar, a hitman, a renegade priest,
a retired spy, but he looks at everyone
with wondering eyes.

The whole story will never be told
but see the fragments you grasp from the air
turn to moments of gold.

All that's left of anyone is a story
and all that's left of a story
is how you tell it.

Sickness sleeplessness worry work visions
of worlds long forgotten by him and other men;
Tinker is a multitude again.

Here and there, up and down, in and out,
passing faces for forty years.
Talk of familiar strangers!

'Yes, I am an addict,' she says, 'and I realise
that addiction is slavery pretending to be
freedom. But yes, I am an addict.'

Tinker walks by the Liffey's edge
through a world of glass and money. Poverty once.
He crosses the Seán O'Casey Bridge.

'There's more cocaine in Dublin now
than almost any city in Europe.
Well, there's the top. And there's over the top.'

She says, 'When I cut the past and the future
out of my life, I can bear
to live now.'

If we could build bridges between each other
as we do over rivers, we might
flow together.

Tinker bows his head before Now,
lets it happen, lets it go
like a childhood dream of Christmas snow.

Now, waking into darkness, Tinker wonders who
advised him in the sea of blood
to swim with D.H. Lawrence and his kangaroo.

Two men walk up to the door, knock promptly.
He opens it.
They shoot him dead, walk away.

'Would you say,' she asks, 'that we live on the most
corrupt little island in the world now
where everything worthwhile is so fragile?'

'There are good dreamers, good dreams,' she says 'but why
do good dreams lead to such ugliness, greed
and the scattering of evil seed?'

In Birmingham, he hears these words again:
'Love is a dream. If you do not dream
you will know a different pain.'

Once, he walked through cities. Now,
cities flash through him
like recognisable faces with forgotten names.

Walking between two Cathedrals, Tinker sees
another old man, dribbling snot,
begging on his knees.

Jonathan Swift walked here through filth.
Was this where he got the notion that eating
roasted babies brought good health?

'They drug themselves to find some change
in their boring lives. Boredom is a huge
challenge for men, women and children.'

'Once, I escaped to South-East Asia,
stayed there, boredom-free, for seven years.
Back at home now, looking at the sea.'

Tinker studies faces in water, trees, clouds.
A few thousand years ago
he'd have created new gods.

Sometimes, when Tinker ponders street faces,
he wonders, what would happen if our minds
danced free of us, and changed places?

A man or a woman is a world.
The problem is how to open a world
and find the country you'd like to live in.

No end to the journeys, is there?
All the journeys are one journey leading
to a moment of almost knowing who you are.

This may not be what it is intended to be
yet all the words and pictures strive
to do what they were born to do: keep lines alive.

Live now, Tinker. Like the fly escaping the light,
like the old book enlightening young eyes,
like the true moment sidestepping lies.

Tinker, where are you going? You're not talking now,
and maybe that's just as well. Drop a line sometime.
You'll always have a story to tell,
something to dream and think and say
that will probe and raggle and find
its own way.

Tinker, when I think of you,
certain moments in this time of lies
ring true.

Who could begin to say what's happening
now? Nobody. Never. However, let's begin
with the majestic cormorant in the brown river.

A stranger walks up to Tinker on the Appian Way.
His face is haggard, his back bent, his hair grey.
He murmurs, 'God bless you and yours', and walks away.